WELCOME!

D1311804

Thank you for purchasing '101 Awesome Activity Book for kids'. This book is a fantastic resource for children as it contains a range of educational games such as mazes, dot to dot, coloring, wordsearch puzzles, math exercises, English and phonics exercises, pattern recognition games etc.

These activities are designed to be both fun and educational, helping children to develop their skills in a range of areas like problem-solving abilities, critical thinking skills, hand-eye coordination, reading , writing and comprehension, numerical and logical skills, and cognitive abilities.

We believe that this activity book will be a valuable addition to your child's learning journey and we hope that they will enjoy the games and puzzles while developing their skills.

THIS BOOK BELONGS TO

_____

THANK YOU GIFT

As a gift to your child, here is a an activity book that you can download , print and enjoy. Simply follow the link to get the gift!

www.pixiepagepress.com/resource

I know that your children will enjoy our activity book and that it will be a valuable addition to their learning journey. I would greatly appreciate it if you could take a moment to leave a review and share your thoughts about the book. Your feedback is essential in helping me improve my products and ensuring that I continue to provide high-quality resources for children. Thank you for your support!

Pixie Page Press.

CONTENT

COLORING

Color the animal and trace the name of the animal

elephant

Color the animal and trace the name of the animal

tortoise

Color the animal and trace the name of the animal

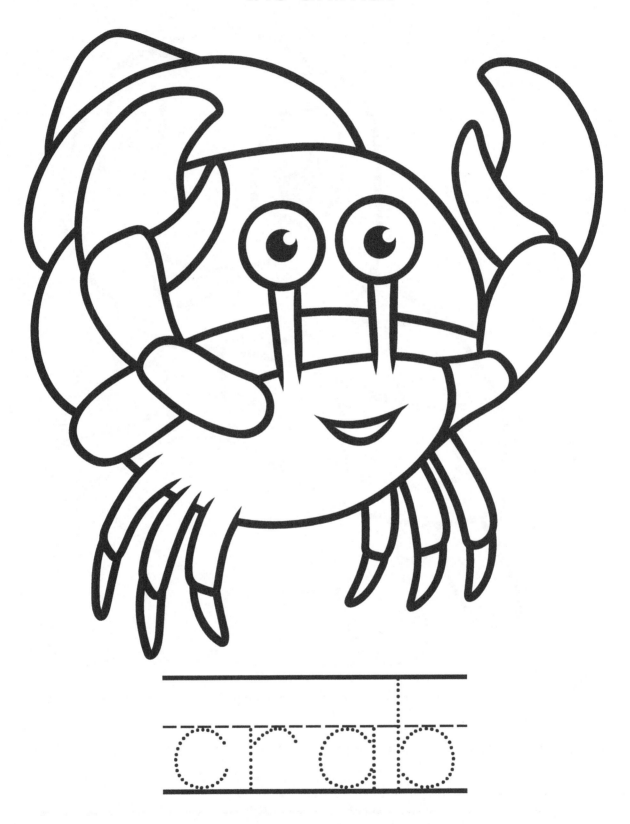

crab

Color the animal and trace the name of the animal

parrot

Color the animal and trace the name of the animal

rabbit

Color the animal and trace the name of the animal

zebra

Color the animal and trace the name of the animal

dog

Color the animal and trace the name of the animal

rhino

Color the animal and trace the name of the animal

lion

Color the animal and trace the name of the animal

penguin

Color the animal and trace the name of the animal

octopus

Color the animal and trace the name of the animal

panda

Color the animal and trace the name of the animal

penguin

DOT TO DOT

1. connect the dots 2. color   3. trace

1. connect the dots   2. color   3. trace

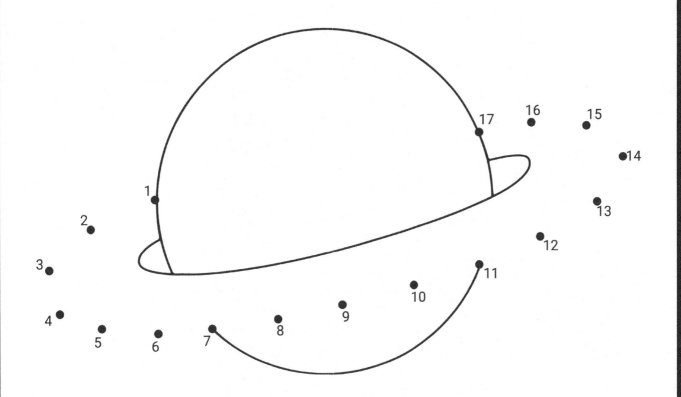

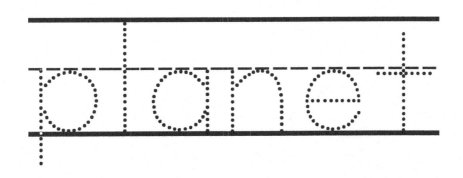

1. connect the dots   2. color   3. trace

1. connect the dots   2. color   3. trace

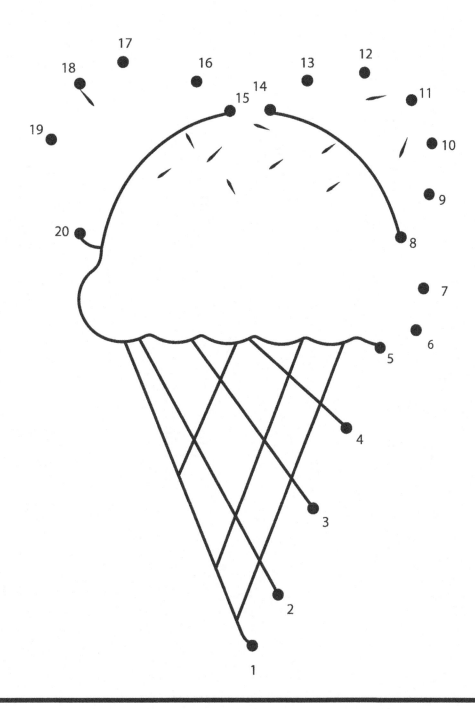

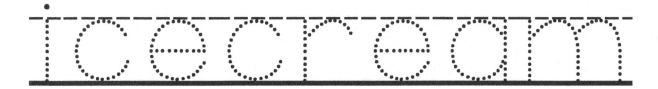

icecream

1. connect the dots   2. color   3. trace

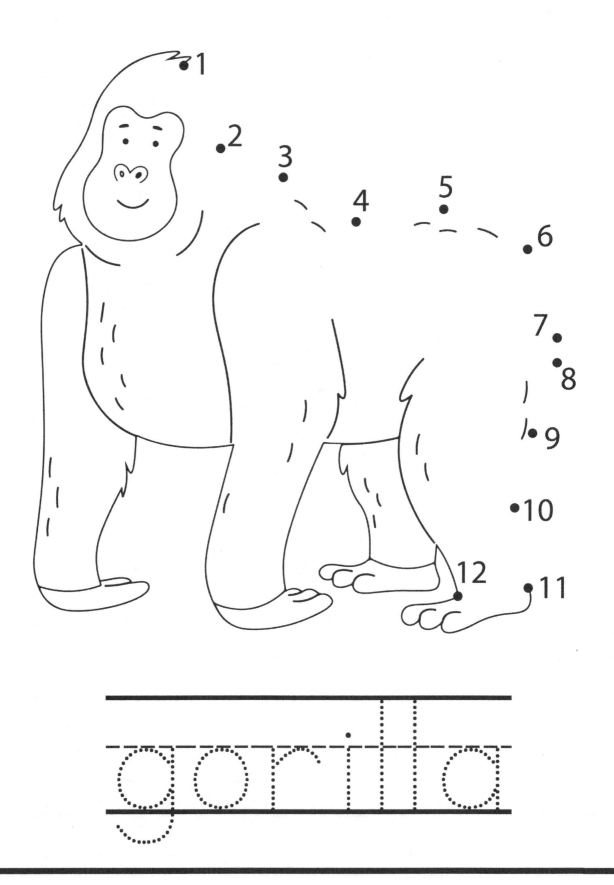

1. connect the dots   2. color   3. trace

strawberry

1. connect the dots   2. color   3. trace

1. connect the dots   2. color   3. trace

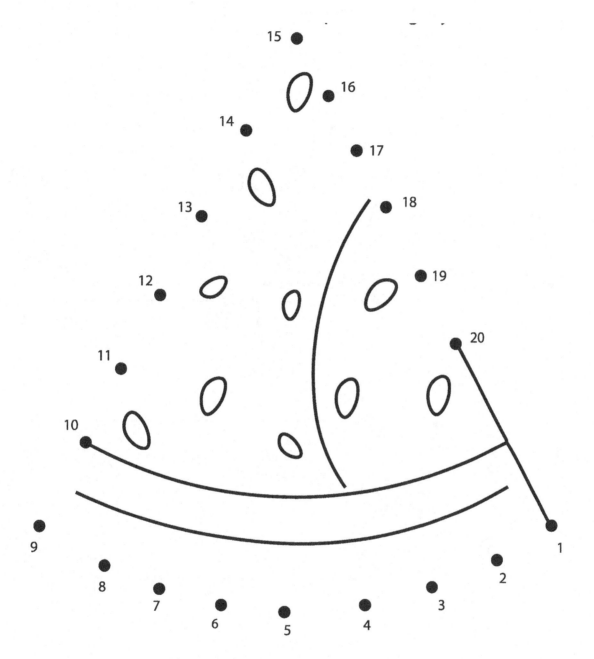

watermelon

1. connect the dots   2. color   3. trace

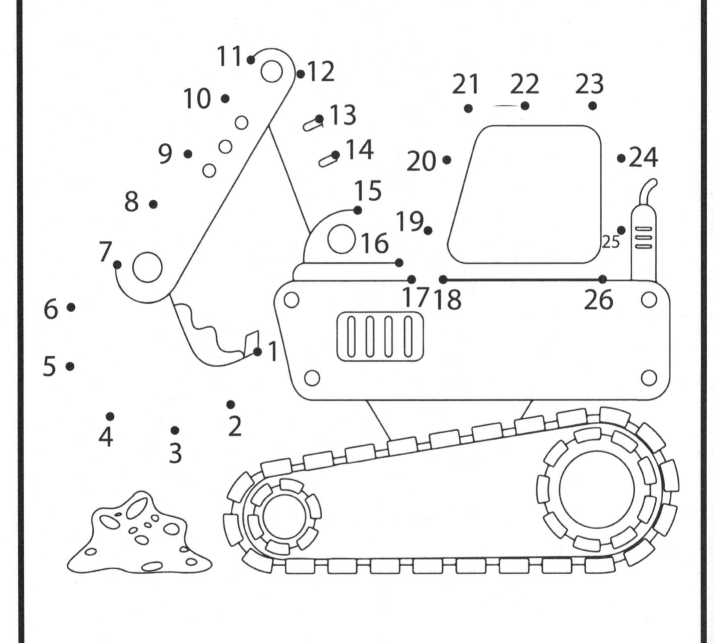

1. connect the dots   2. color   3. trace

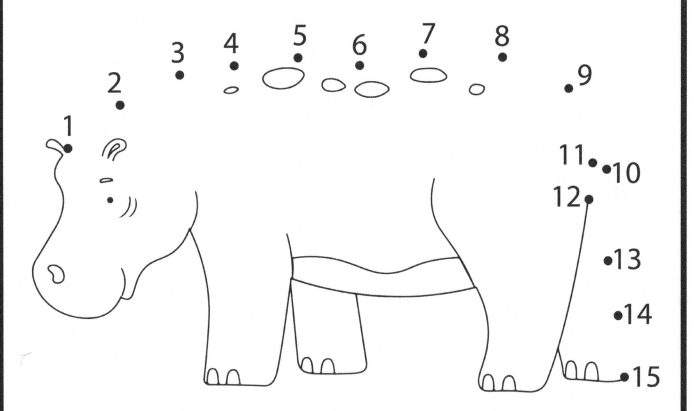

hippopotamus

1. connect the dots   2. color   3. trace

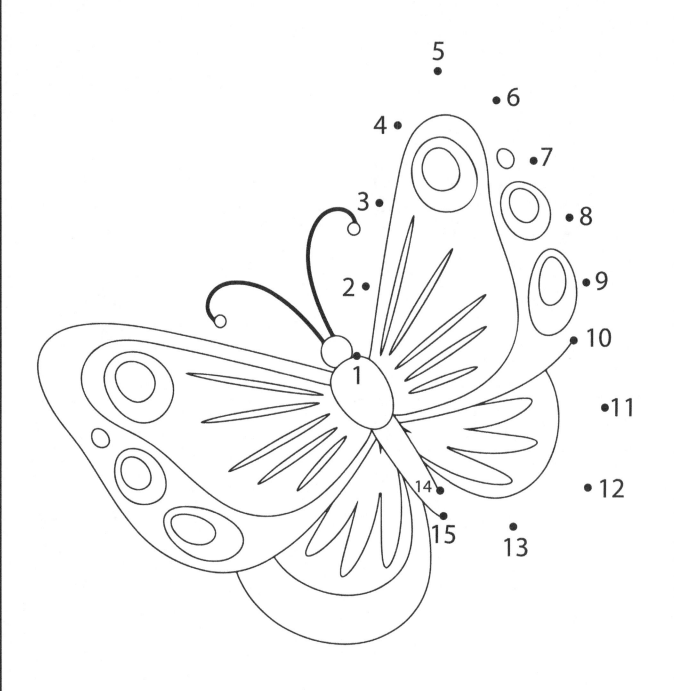

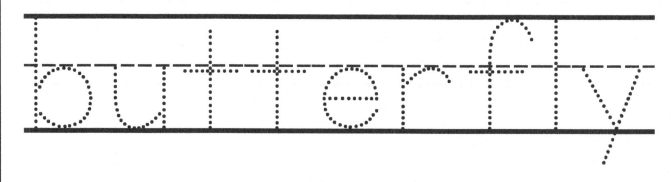

1. connect the dots 2. color   3. trace

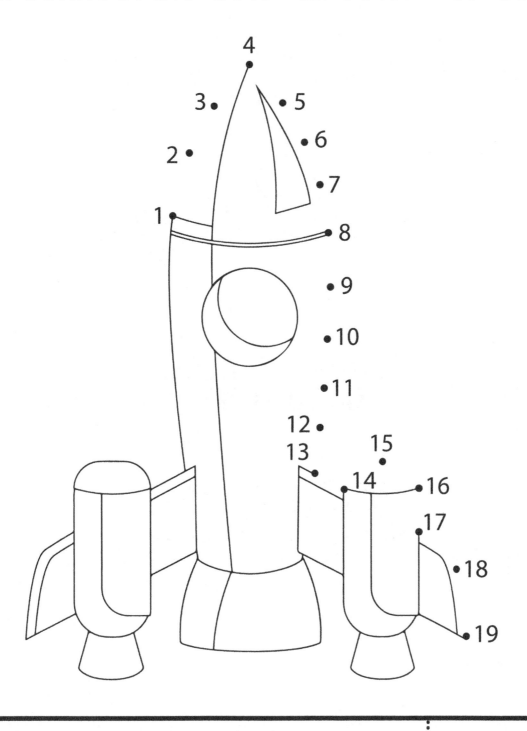

MATHS

GAMES

Count the objects and write the numbers(1-10) in the box

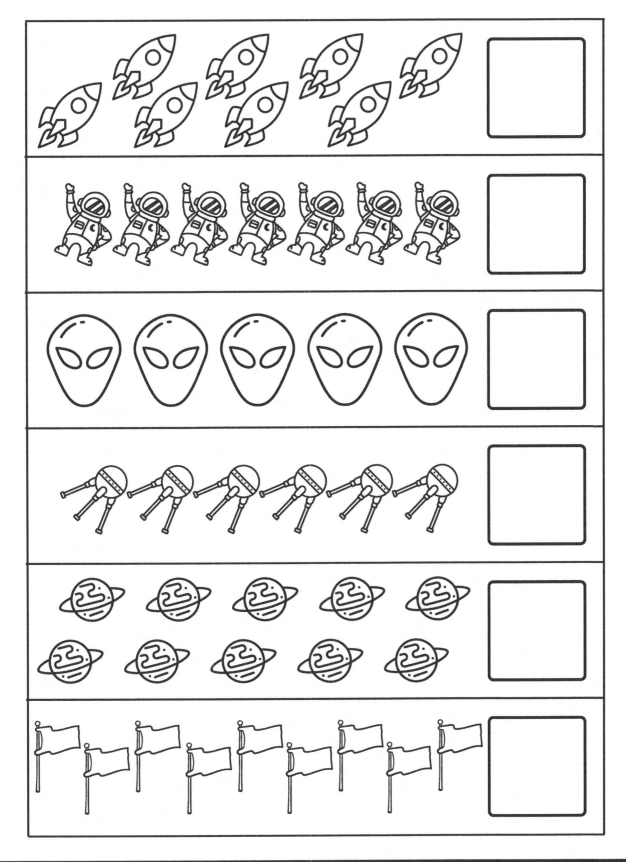

Count the objects and write the numbers (11-20) in the box

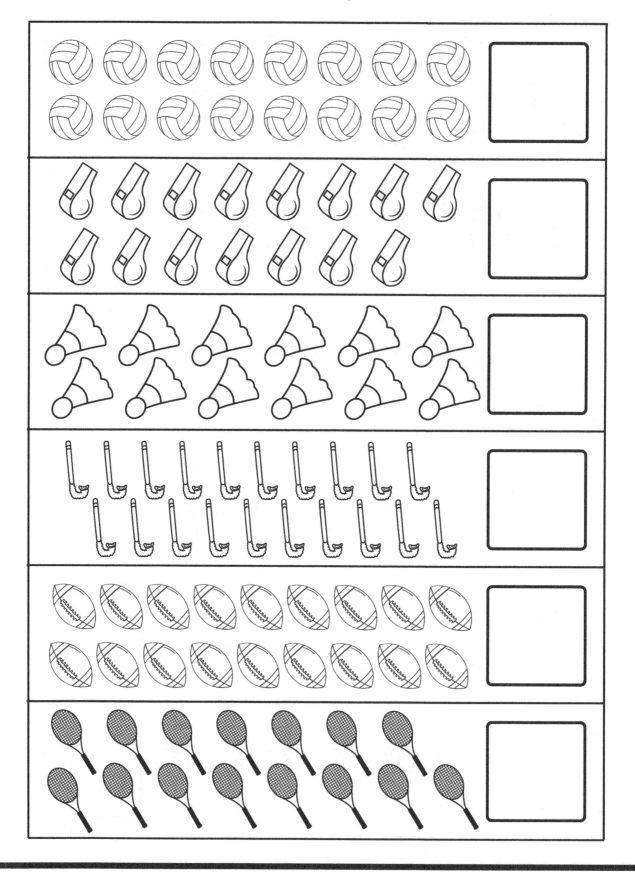

Count the objects then add with the numbers. Write the answer inside the box provided.

⭐⭐⭐ + 6 = _

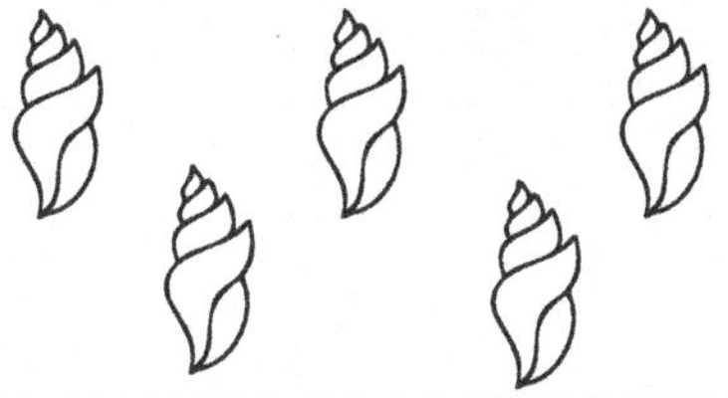

🐚🐚🐚🐚🐚 + 8 = _

🪼🪼🪼🪼🪼 + _ = 9

🦄🦄🦄🦄 + 7 = _

🐋🐋🐋 + _ = 12

Math Drills : Addition

```
  6        2        9        7        0
+ 3      + 5      + 3      + 1      + 8
----     ----     ----     ----     ----
```

```
  9        6        3        7        1
+ 2      + 6      + 4      + 8      + 5
----     ----              ----     ----
```

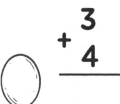

```
  4        5        7        4        2
+ 0      + 3      + 7      + 9      + 6
----     ----     ----     ----     ----
```

```
  4        6        6        8        4
+ 7      + 9      + 3      + 9      + 2
----     ----     ----     ----     ----
```

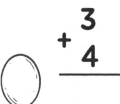

```
  3        6        8        7        9
+ 3      + 4      + 6      + 3      + 9
----     ----     ----     ----     ----
```

Math Drills : Addition

Draw extra apples on the tree to help solve the equations:

3 + 6 =

4 + 3 =

7 + 2 =

1 + 9 =

Count the image. Draw a line between the total number of images on each box and the number on the right.

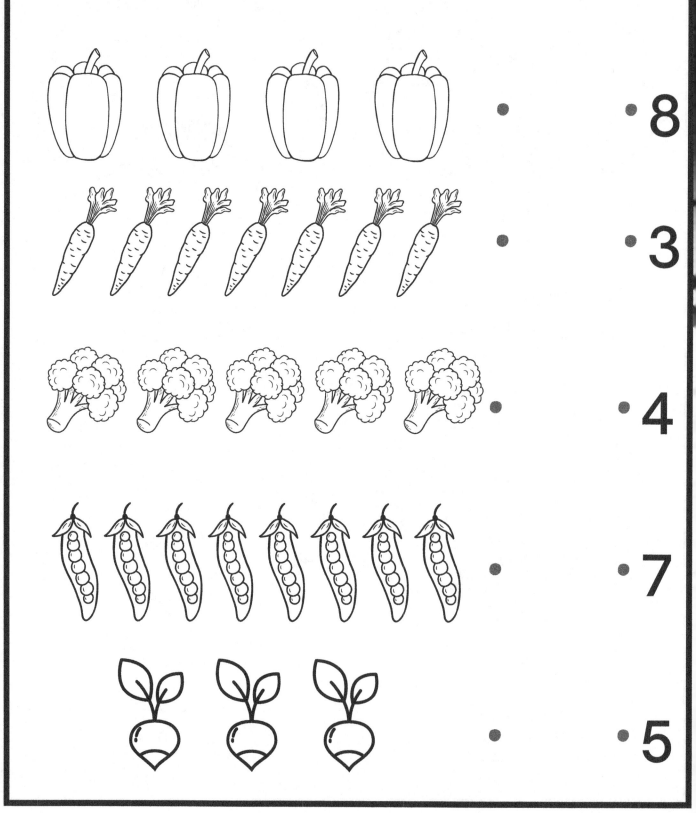

Count the image. Draw a line between the total number of images on each box and the number on the right.

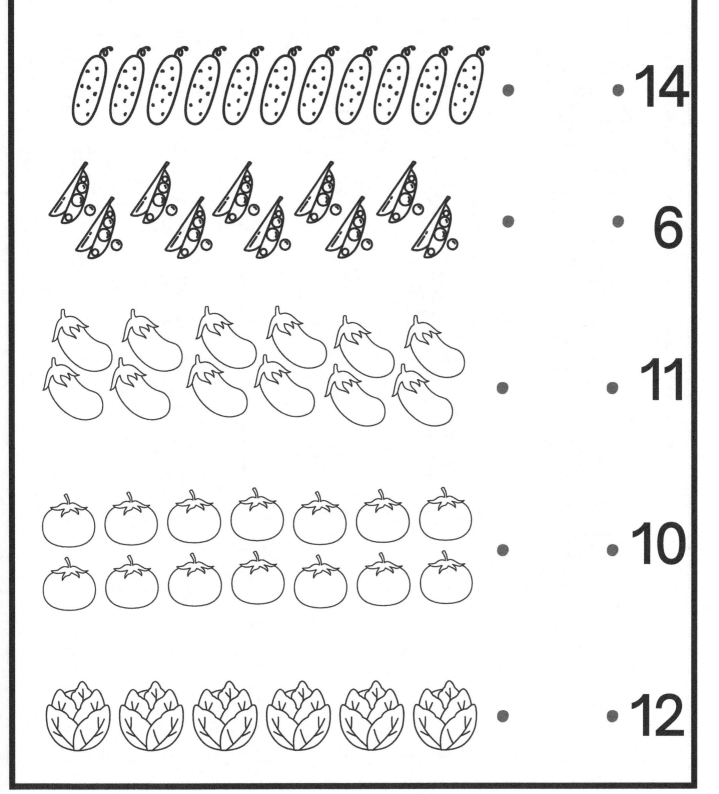

How many objects are there? Count and write

CUT & PASTE

Cut, sort and paste the pictures under
the correct word.
Color the pictures and write each word
on your own.

angel	bat	cookie	desk

----

elephant	fan	girl	hand

Can you complete each Pattern? Cut and glue

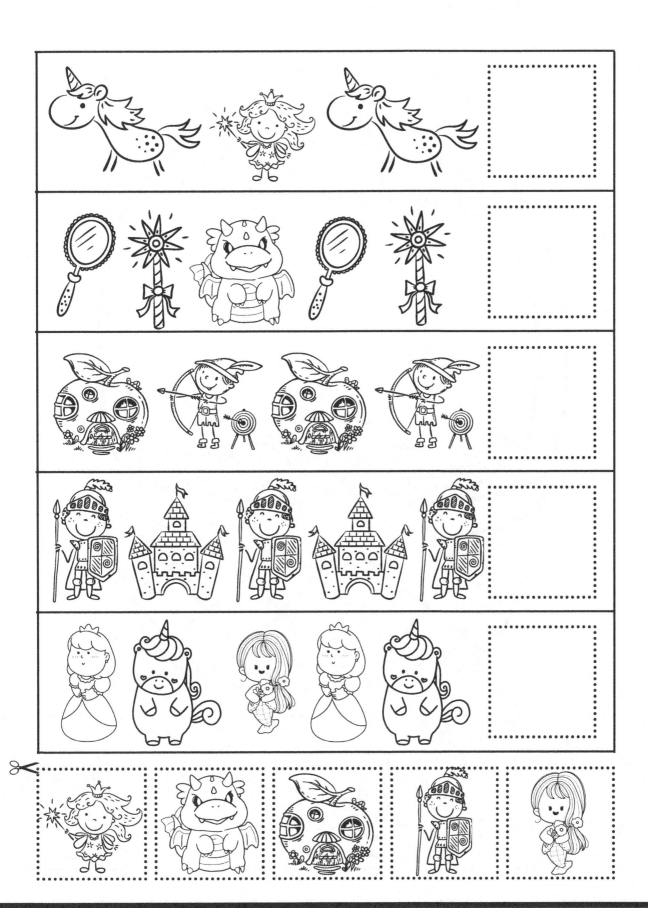

Put the fruits in the basket

Cut the giraffe's
body parts and
place on the body

Cut and paste the picture to match each word family "u", then color the image.

bus	hut	sun
jug	nut	cup

✂ ···

Cut the dinosaurs and place them in the forest below

Cut, sort and paste the pictures under
the correct word.
Color the pictures and write each word
on your own.

ant	ball	cow	dog

_____   _____
_____   _____
_____   _____

egg	fish	goat	house

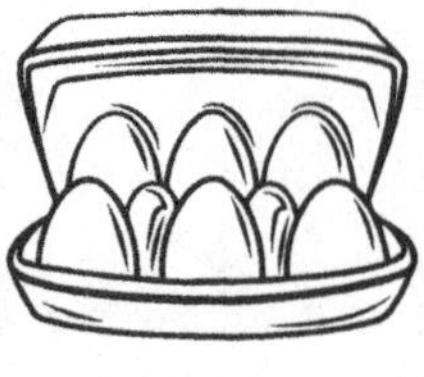

_____   _____
_____   _____
_____   _____

Cut the sea creatures and place them in the ocean below

Cut and paste the picture to match each word family "a", then color the image.

cat	hat	mat
rat	dad	pan

✂ ··

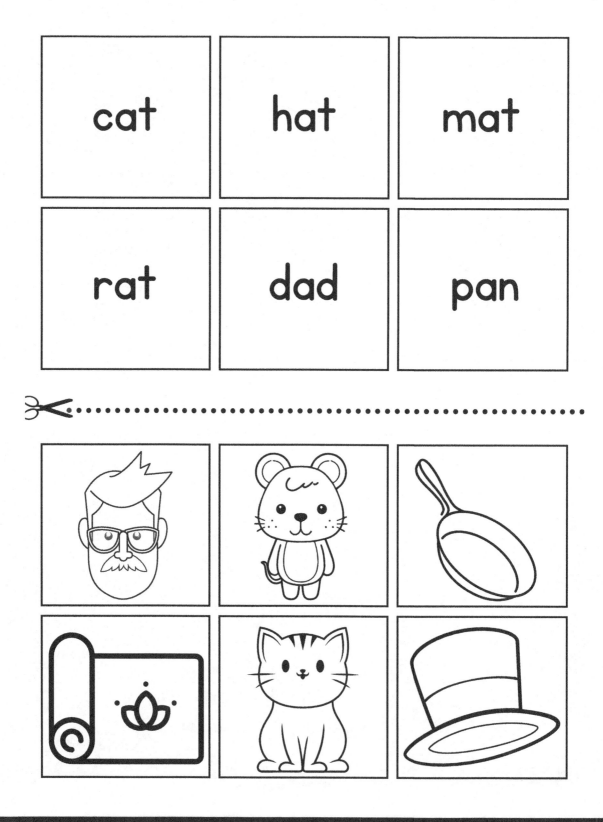

PHONICS

Write the correct vowel to complete each word.

a   e   i   o   u

b __ll   d __ g   m __on

c __ r   f __sh   tre __

b __rd   st __r   b __by

Read the comprehension, color the objects, &
answer the questions

Read the story :

Tommy went to the zoo.
He saw a lion, a tiger and a
monKey.
Tommy had a fun day.

Color:

Fill In the answer:

Who went to the zoo?
What animals did he see at the zoo?
Did Tommy have a fun day at the
zoo?

Color the object in each group that does not start with the same letter

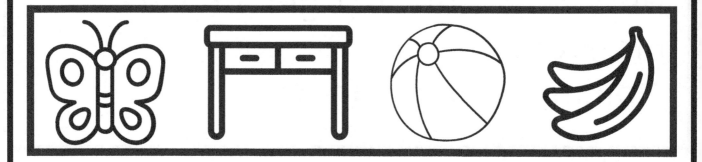

Look at the picture, unscramble the word and color the picture

eeb _____

oumes _____

geg _____

nus _____

Read the comprehension, color the objects, & answer the questions

Read the story :

Sarah and Jake went to the beach. They played in the sand and built sandcastles. They swam in the ocean and saw colorful fish. What a day!

Color:

Fill In the answer:

Who went to the beach?
What did they do at the beach?
what did they see while swimming?

Write the correct vowel to complete each word.

| a | e | i | o | u |

b __ t

c __ ke

b __ ok

t __ y

tr __ in

fr __ g

mug

cl __ ck

d __ ll

Look at the picture, unscramble the word and color the picture

papel

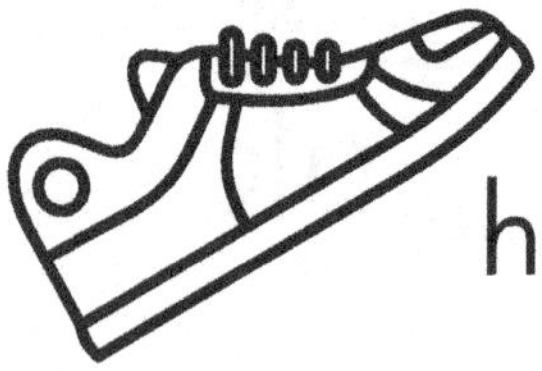

_____

heos

_____

osonp

_____

ctkru

_____

Read the sentences and color the correct object.

I see an orange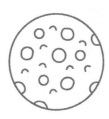

I see an egg

I see a butterfly

I see a house

I see a flower

COLOR BY

NUMBER

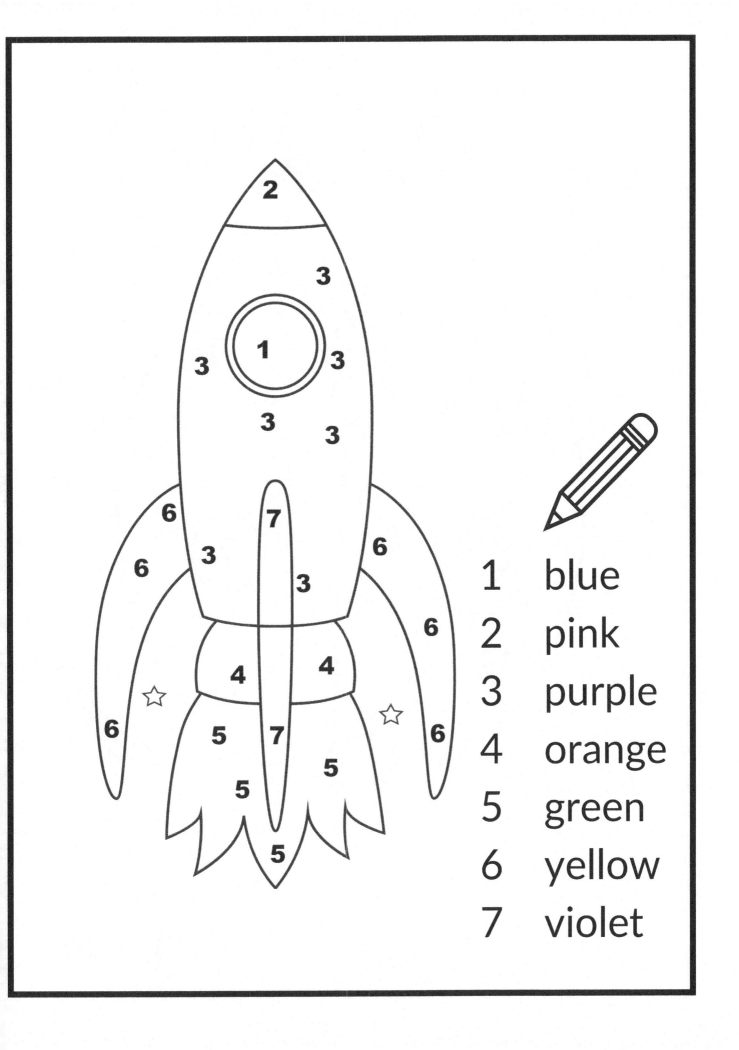

1 blue
2 pink
3 purple
4 orange
5 green
6 yellow
7 violet

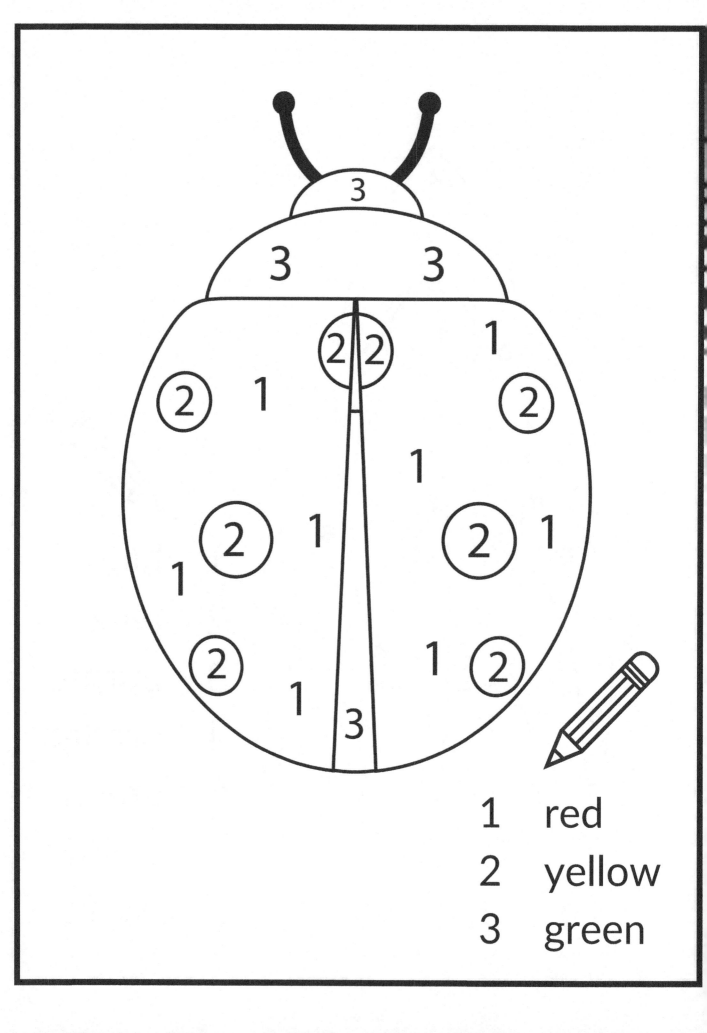

1   red

2   yellow

3   green

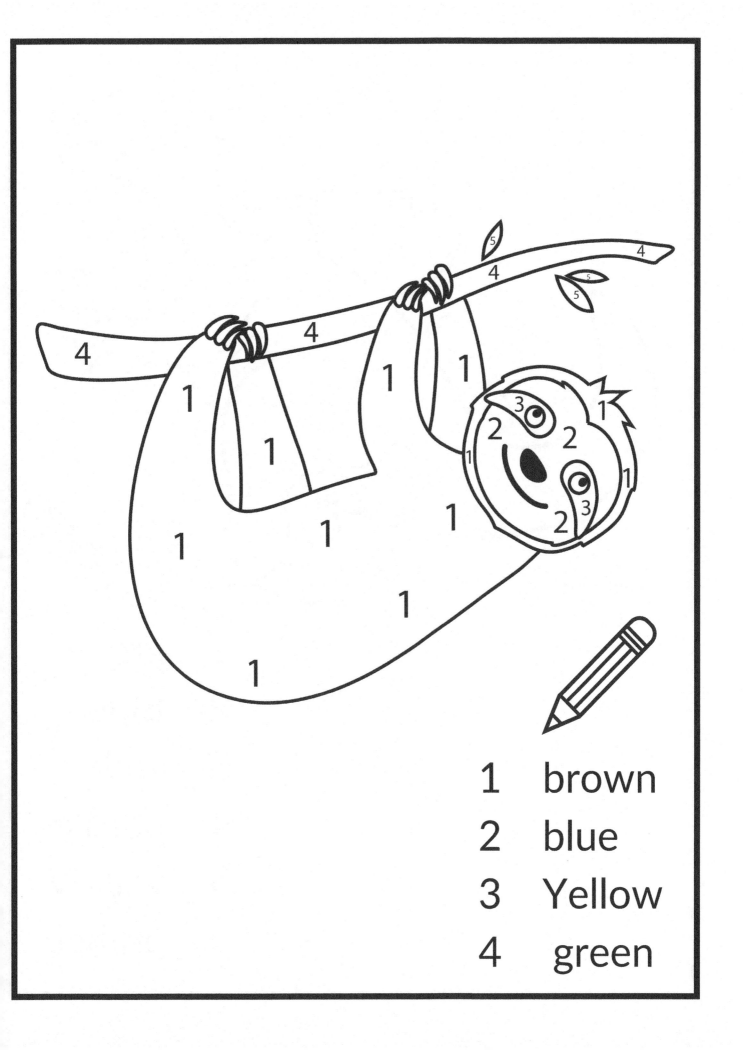

1 brown
2 blue
3 Yellow
4 green

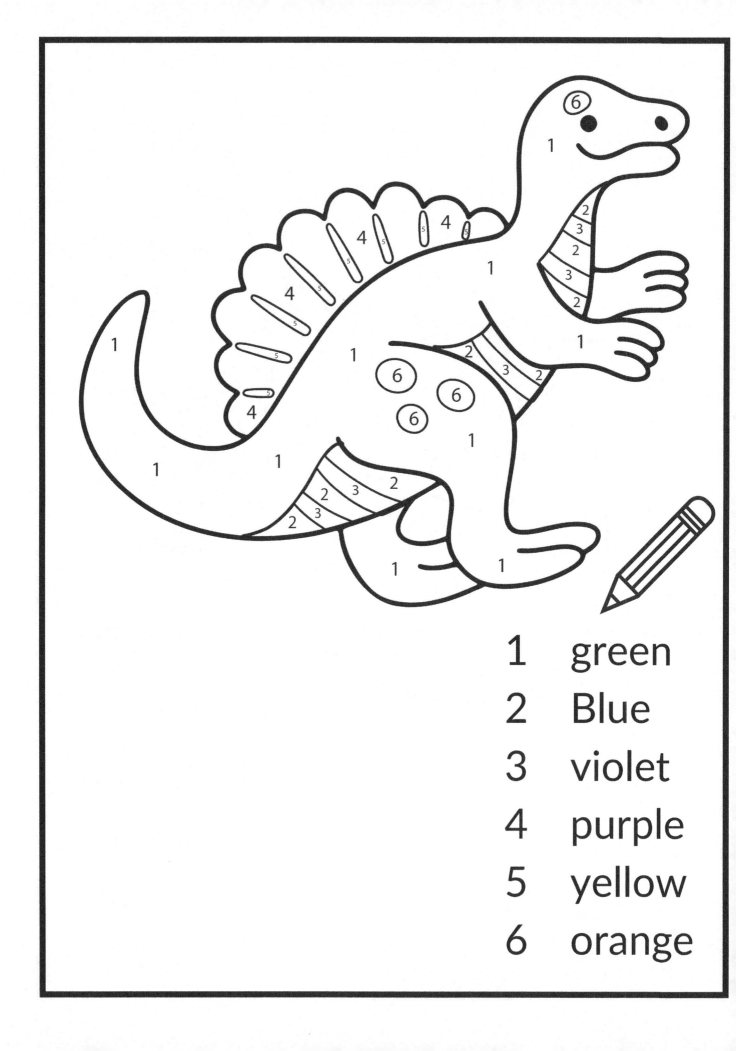

1 green
2 Blue
3 violet
4 purple
5 yellow
6 orange

1 Pink
2 yellow
3 red
4 purple
5 blue

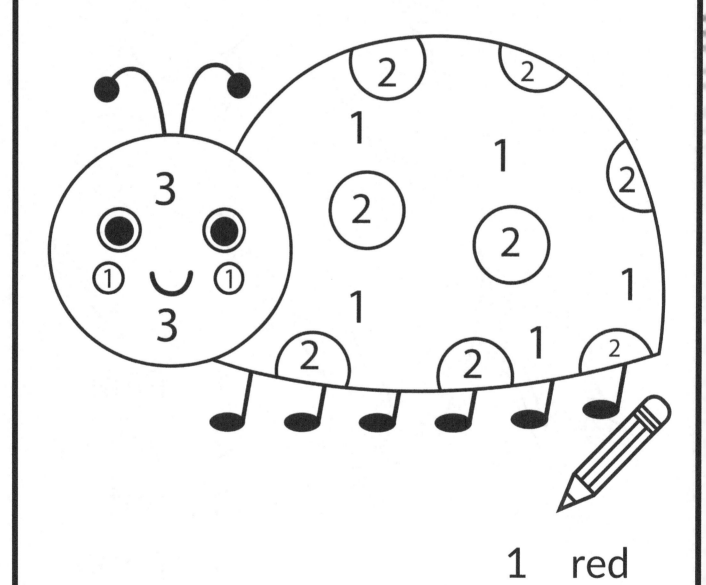

1   red

2   black

3   yellow

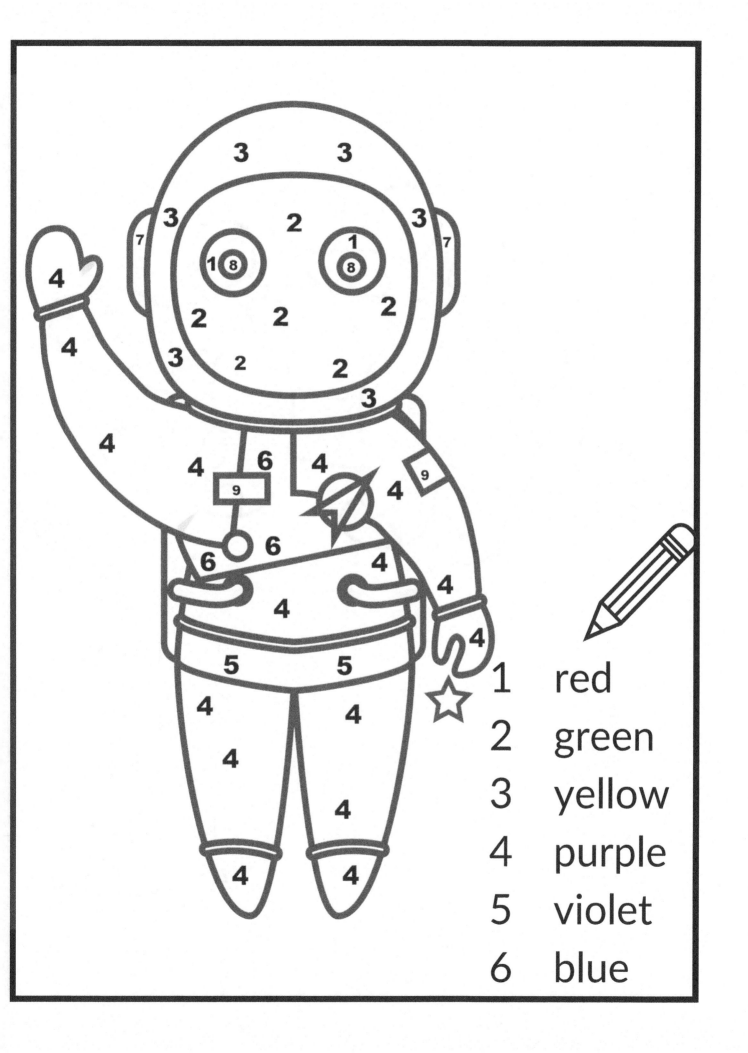

1 red
2 green
3 yellow
4 purple
5 violet
6 blue

1   brown

2   green

3   red

4   blue

5   yellow

1 Pink
2 Blue
3 Yellow

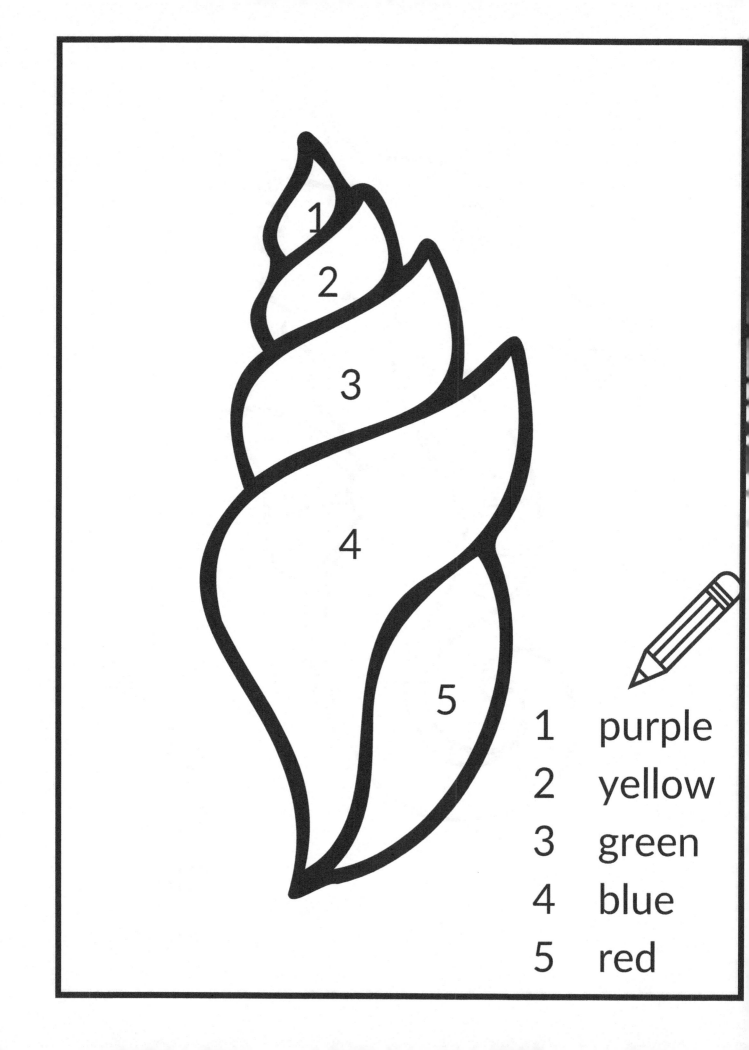

1　purple
2　yellow
3　green
4　blue
5　red

1   green

2   orange

3   violet

4   red

5   blue

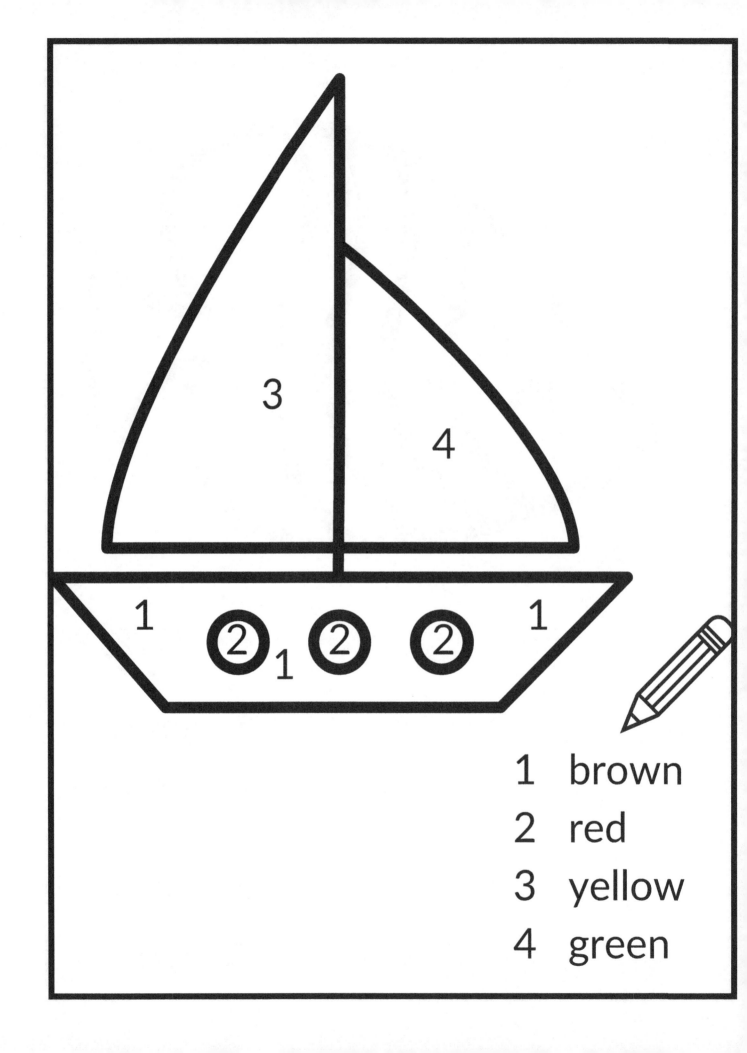

1 brown
2 red
3 yellow
4 green

MAZE

Find the fastest way for the car to get to school

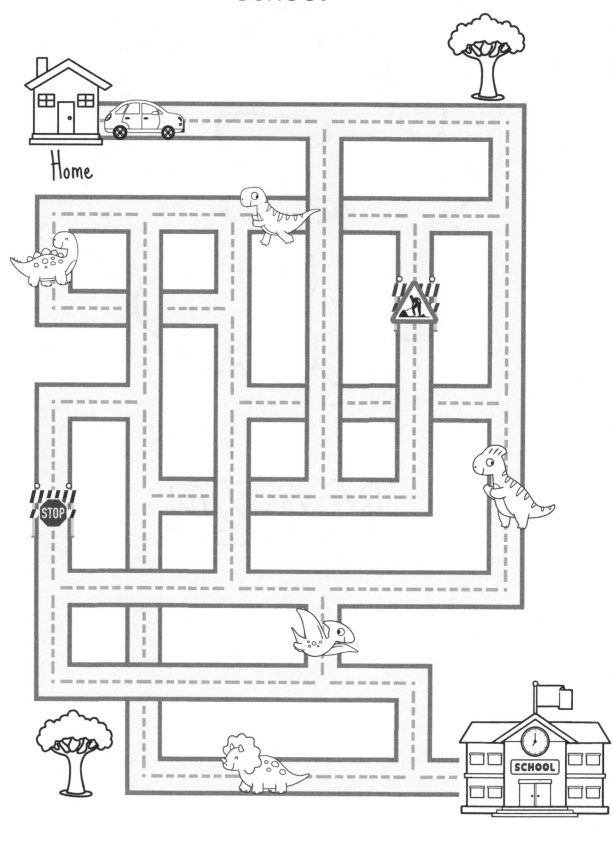

Help the astronaut find his spaceship

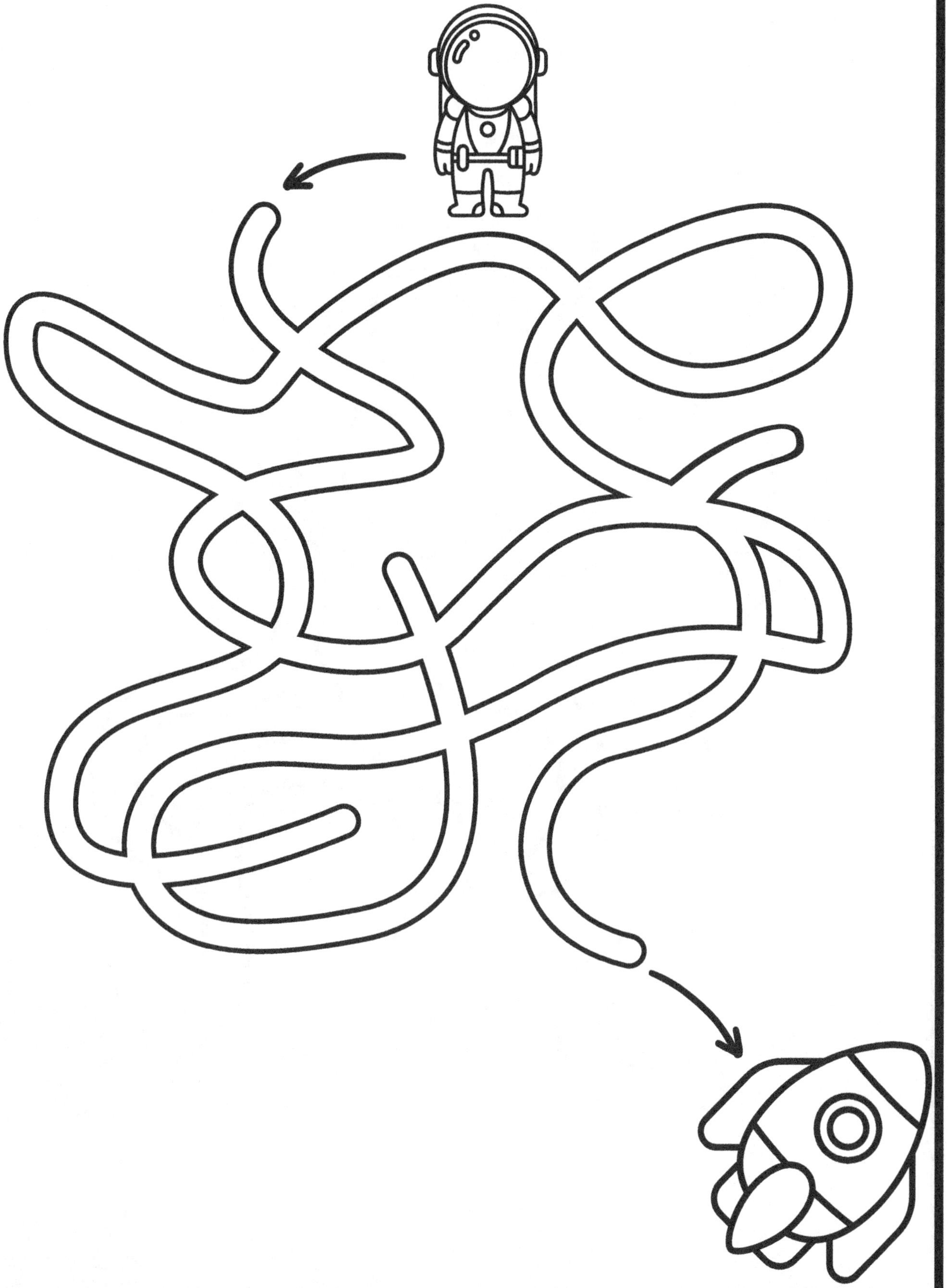

Help the girl find her kite

How many pineapples can the boy put in his basket, following the right path?

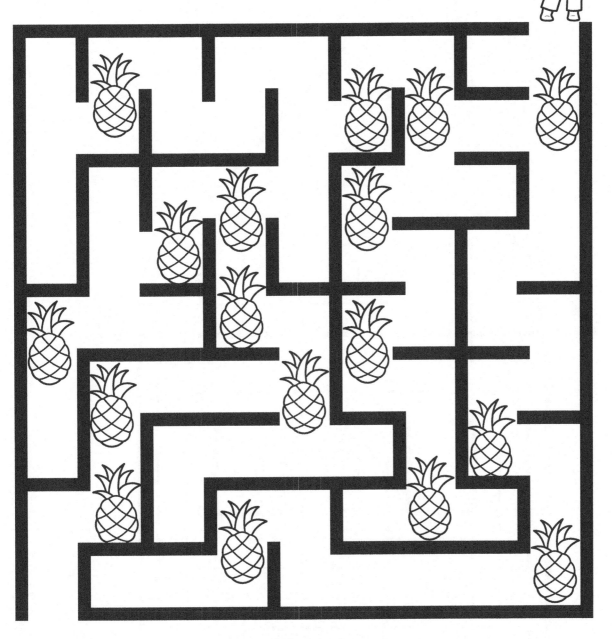

Number of Pineapples	

Help the cat find the mouse!

Find the safest way for the baby monkey to get to his mother

Help the rabbit find the apple tree

Help the bee find her beehive!

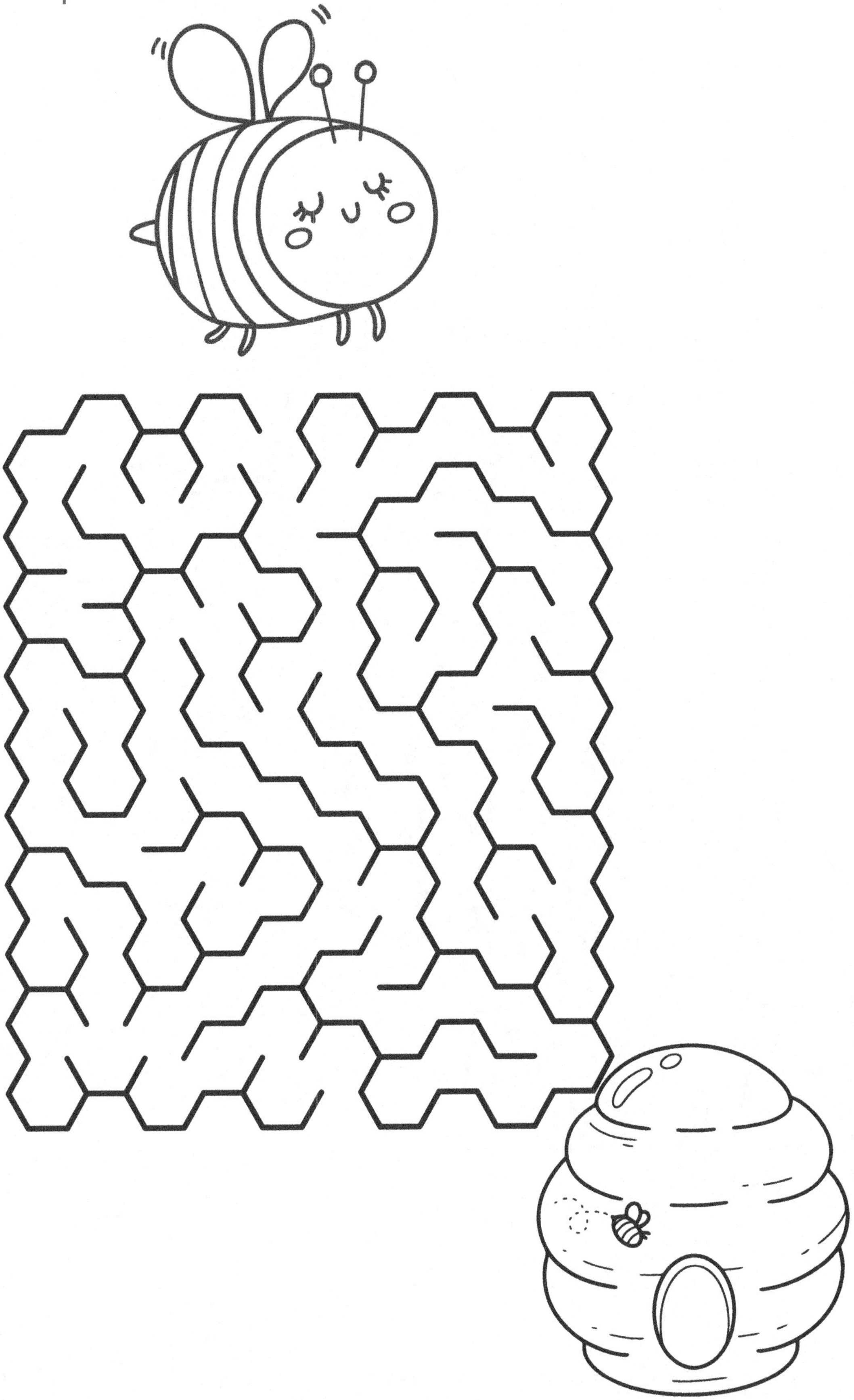

Help the princess go to her castle

Help the kids find the ice cream shop

Help the bunny find his carrots

Help the bird find her nest

Help the baby find his bottle

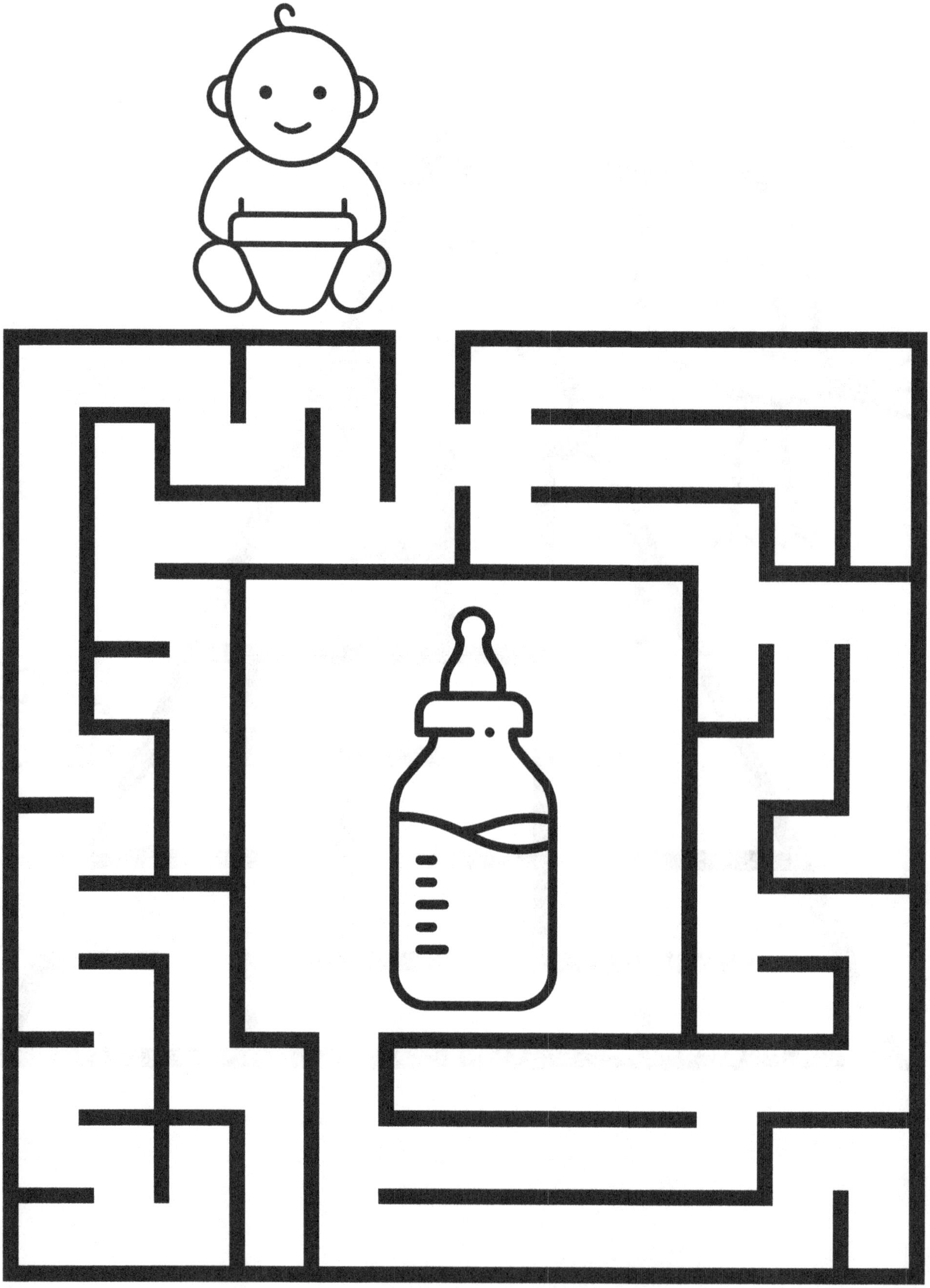

PATTERN

RECOGNITION

Match the birds with their shadows by drawing a line.

Trace, draw and color the shapes

Draw the other half of each object and then color it

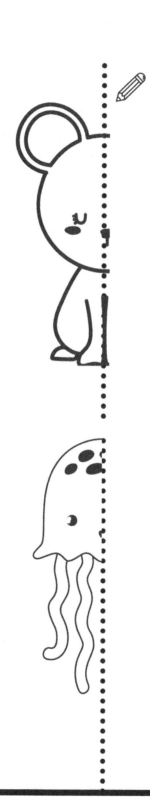

Color all the hearts PINK, all the circles ORANGE and the squares BLUE.

Match the animals with their shadows by drawing a line.

Connect the dots to match the words on the left to its figure on the right.

Rectangle •   • ☐

Square •   • ▭

Circle •   • ○

Star •   • △

Triangle •   • ☆

Connect the pictures to their matching shape.

Draw the other half of the insect and then color it

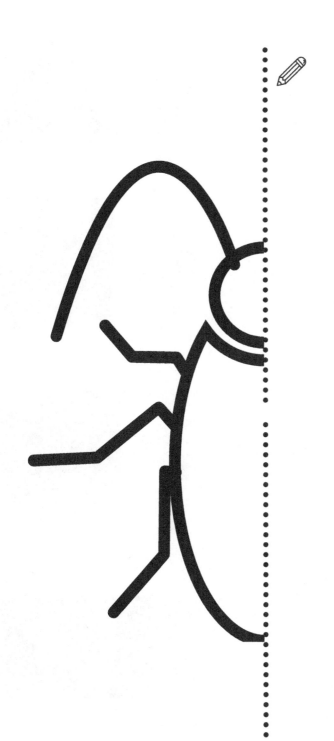

Connect the pictures to their matching shape.

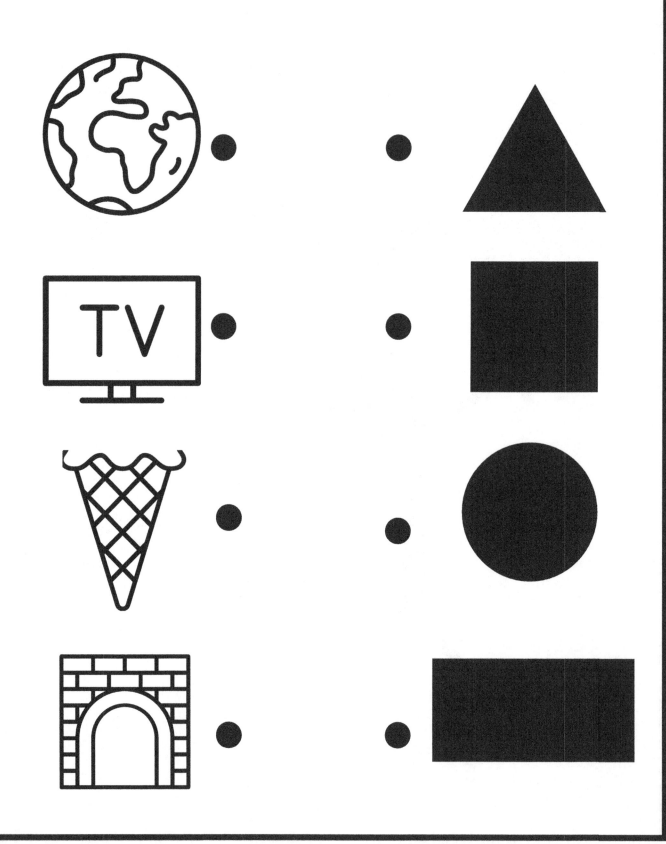

Draw the other half of the insect and then color it

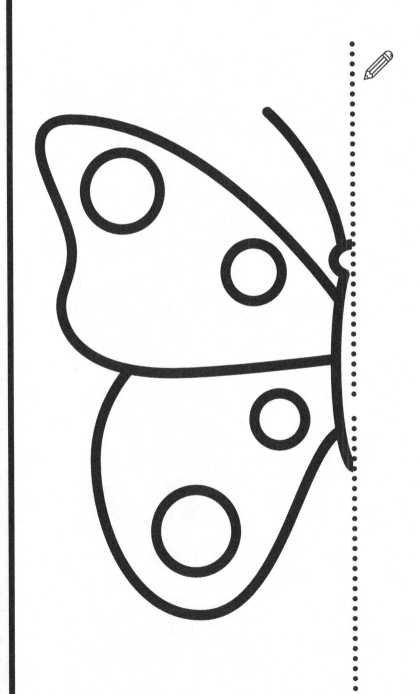

Match the animals with their shadows by drawing a line.

SIGHTWORD

WORDSEARCH

can you find the sight-words in the puzzle below?

Puzzle #1

W	C	Y	N	B	Z	M	R
H	W	A	A	G	E	W	Q
I	R	Q	L	M	O	R	Z
C	I	J	O	L	E	O	Y
H	T	C	U	T	E	A	Z
Q	E	N	A	U	B	D	O
Q	Q	W	W	A	W	N	Z
C	W	L	Y	R	O	S	X

CALLED   COME

WATER   WHICH

WRITE

can you find the sight-words in the puzzle below?

Puzzle #2

K	F	T	U	P	J	O	H
F	C	C	U	N	A	C	F
A	V	O	T	F	A	R	A
W	G	I	I	E	D	U	T
W	I	X	J	S	I	M	B
E	I	N	I	F	Q	A	R
M	A	H	D	J	P	Y	K
Q	G	R	S	O	M	E	E

EACH   HIS

MAY   PART

SOME

can you find the sight-words in the puzzle below?

Puzzle #3

```
V   B   L   Z   C   W   F   U

O   R   Q   W   H   A   S   G

N   R   I   N   T   O   M   F

K   Y   B   B   R   O   A   H

D   Q   D   U   D   Q   K   Q

Z   V   I   P   T   X   E   G

O   D   D   C   F   E   C   H

W   M   U   Z   S   Z   U   V
```

BUT   DID
HAS   INTO
MAKE

can you find the sight-words in the puzzle below?

Puzzle #4

E	E	I	M	K	B	T	B
O	V	T	E	W	M	H	A
Q	T	S	P	D	J	E	K
X	H	M	H	L	T	I	B
H	A	U	Y	W	S	R	R
E	T	M	O	M	Q	X	H
R	P	M	U	E	S	S	U
M	F	N	R	G	U	H	F

HER   ITS

THAT   THEIR

YOUR

can you find the sight-words in the puzzle below?

Puzzle #5

```
G   R   U   E   S   O   I   X

L   X   S   L   G   S   R   A

Y   S   B   A   W   L   N   Q

L   H   J   Y   F   Q   V   P

A   O   A   B   H   O   Q   P

Q   N   N   D   W   I   R   G

D   P   S   G   X   X   M   Q

R   W   O   R   D   S   P   K
```

FOR   HAD
HIM   LONG
WORDS

can you find the sight-words in the puzzle below?

Puzzle #6

C	E	U	D	A	Y	A	U
I	S	T	I	M	E	X	S
E	I	S	N	H	P	A	P
J	G	R	H	N	N	B	A
I	B	D	O	E	I	O	N
L	G	S	N	B	W	O	T
Z	H	A	V	E	D	U	W
F	K	F	T	T	E	K	J

DAY   HAVE

NOT   SHE

TIME

can you find the sight-words in the puzzle below?

Puzzle #7

```
W   X   R   J   I   E   M   I
W   L   U   Z   N   X   M   M
B   E   E   N   A   O   L   V
A   Z   J   Z   R   T   W   L
F   G   L   N   E   F   K   B
T   O   Y   X   G   S   O   A
F   Q   R   S   A   I   D   Y
K   T   H   A   N   U   S   T
```

ARE   BEEN
NOW   SAID
THAN

can you find the sight-words in the puzzle below?

Puzzle #8

H	A	I	T	C	S	X	P
N	R	O	Q	A	V	L	Q
P	W	W	B	N	C	Z	E
S	Y	H	I	O	U	T	I
M	T	D	E	O	W	F	J
O	N	H	A	N	O	Y	J
R	C	R	E	E	P	S	M
E	C	M	T	K	S	Q	X

CAN   MORE

OUT   THE

WHEN

can you find the sight-words in the puzzle below?

Puzzle #9

F	U	A	F	V	X	L	Y
R	D	U	I	L	T	B	A
G	O	K	J	E	H	A	G
B	W	V	S	C	E	L	D
H	N	U	T	O	N	L	N
C	Y	E	T	Q	K	V	Z
F	G	M	P	G	G	S	G
R	E	R	L	X	U	M	X

ALL   DOWN
GET   THEN
USE

can you find the sight-words in the puzzle below?

Puzzle #10

F	S	E	I	J	S	F	I
R	E	Z	Y	K	Q	I	Z
S	P	X	P	H	G	R	N
V	Y	S	E	F	O	S	M
G	Y	O	U	B	I	T	S
A	Y	M	A	N	Y	N	L
A	R	U	K	P	P	B	D
K	G	S	W	H	X	H	V

FIND
MANY
YOU

FIRST
SEE

can you find the sight-words in the puzzle below?

Puzzle #11

O	M	O	T	H	E	R	H
G	H	R	G	Y	T	N	C
P	Z	N	U	P	F	D	S
Z	U	K	F	S	K	B	T
T	I	X	L	R	J	U	Q
V	K	E	T	O	O	Q	J
M	A	D	E	B	O	M	F
Q	Y	S	A	R	X	K	V

ABOUT   FROM
LOOK   MADE
OTHER

can you find the sight-words in the puzzle below?

Puzzle #12

D	L	G	E	T	D	W	E
A	N	X	W	E	O	R	Q
Z	A	I	H	H	E	R	R
J	D	V	A	H	W	V	E
F	Q	V	T	U	I	B	W
T	W	O	P	M	T	J	A
L	K	T	U	N	H	J	K
Z	K	Z	B	V	J	C	C

HOW   THERE
TWO   WHAT
WITH

can you find the sight-words in the puzzle below?

Puzzle #13

E	W	O	J	C	H	S	Y
K	X	W	A	X	S	R	L
B	F	P	T	H	E	M	W
F	N	W	E	W	I	S	E
F	A	W	T	O	V	Z	R
W	W	A	Y	O	P	Y	E
A	S	S	K	Q	I	L	X
C	N	W	T	Q	R	X	E

PEOPLE   THEM

WAS   WAY

WERE

can you find the sight-words in the puzzle below?

Puzzle #14

W	T	N	C	J	R	U	N
E	H	L	U	H	M	I	H
T	G	I	M	M	D	U	D
J	H	K	L	L	B	N	T
M	A	E	U	H	A	E	T
Q	V	O	S	F	D	X	R
Z	W	A	K	E	A	P	F
Y	M	S	K	Y	J	Q	Z

AND   LIKE

NUMBER   THESE

WOULD

can you find the sight-words in the puzzle below?

Puzzle #15

```
C   G   F   J   Z   D   L   V

A   C   O   U   L   D   Z   W

X   M   T   T   H   E   Y   H

T   I   H   U   P   H   H   O

E   B   I   E   P   J   S   E

G   F   S   I   C   D   K   P

H   U   I   F   W   I   L   L

Z   M   S   J   U   W   U   A
```

COULD   THEY
THIS   WHO
WILL

WORDSEARCH SOLUTIONS

Puzzle #1 - Solution

W	C	Y	N	B	Z	M	R
H	W	A	A	G	E	W	Q
I	R	Q	L	M	O	R	Z
C	I	J	O	L	E	O	Y
H	T	C	U	T	E	A	Z
Q	E	N	A	U	B	D	O
Q	Q	W	W	A	W	N	Z
C	W	L	Y	R	O	S	X

Puzzle #2 - Solution

K	F	T	U	P	J	O	H
F	C	C	U	N	A	C	F
A	V	O	T	F	A	R	A
W	G	I	I	E	D	U	T
W	I	X	J	S	I	M	B
E	I	N	I	F	Q	A	R
M	A	H	D	J	P	Y	K
Q	G	R	S	O	M	E	E

Puzzle #3 - Solution

V	B	L	Z	C	W	F	U
O	R	Q	W	H	A	S	G
N	R	I	N	T	O	M	F
K	Y	B	B	R	O	A	H
D	Q	D	U	D	Q	K	Q
Z	V	I	P	T	X	E	G
O	D	D	C	F	E	C	H
W	M	U	Z	S	Z	U	V

Puzzle #4 - Solution

E	E	I	M	K	B	T	B
O	V	T	E	W	M	H	A
Q	T	S	P	D	J	E	K
X	H	M	H	L	T	I	B
H	A	U	Y	W	S	R	R
E	T	M	O	M	Q	X	H
R	P	M	U	E	S	S	U
M	F	N	R	G	U	H	F

Puzzle #5 - Solution

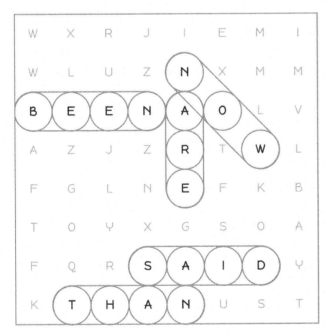

Puzzle #6 - Solution

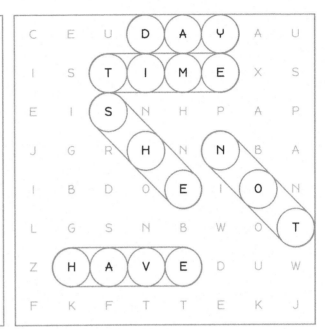

Puzzle #7 - Solution

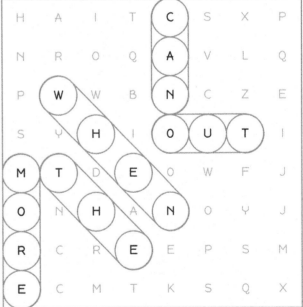

Puzzle #8 - Solution

Puzzle #9 - Solution

Puzzle #10 - Solution

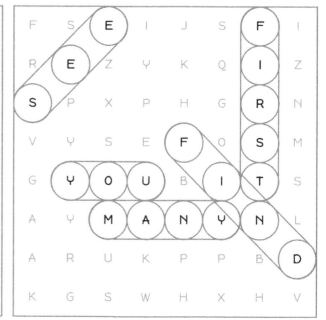

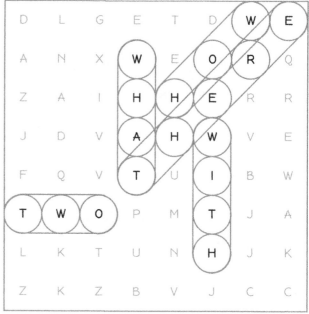

Puzzle #11 - Solution

Puzzle #12 - Solution

Puzzle #13 - Solution

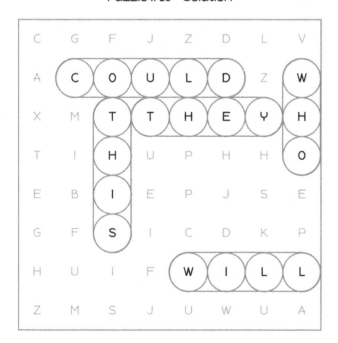

Puzzle #14 - Solution

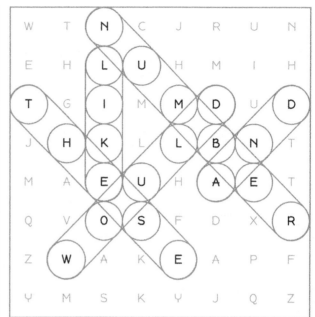

Puzzle #15 - Solution

C	G	F	J	Z	D	L	V
A	C	O	U	L	D	Z	W
X	M	T	T	H	E	Y	H
T	I	H	U	P	H	H	O
E	B	I	E	P	J	S	E
G	F	S	I	C	D	K	P
H	U	I	F	W	I	L	L
Z	M	S	J	U	W	U	A

Made in the USA
Coppell, TX
19 June 2023

18263790R00066